50 Cent

by Z.B. Hill

Superstars of Hip-Hop

Alicia Keys

Beyoncé

Black Eyed Peas

Ciara

Dr. Dre

Drake

Eminem

50 Cent

Flo Rida

Hip Hop:
A Short History

Jay-Z

Kanye West

Lil Wayne

LL Cool J

Ludacris

Mary J. Blige

Notorious B.I.G.

Rihanna

Sean "Diddy" Combs

Snoop Dogg

T.I.

T-Pain

Timbaland

Tupac

Usher

50 Cent

WITHDRAWN

by Z.B. Hill

Mason Crest

50 Cent

Mason Crest
370 Reed Road
Broomall, Pennsylvania 19008
www.masoncrest.com

Printed and bound in the United States of America.

First printing
9 8 7 6 5 4 3 2 1

Library of Congress Cataloging-in-Publication Data

Hill, Z. B.
  50 Cent / by Z.B. Hill.
     p. cm. – (Superstars of hip-hop)
  Includes index.
  ISBN 978-1-4222-2509-7 (hardcover) – ISBN 978-1-4222-2508-0 (series hardcover) – ISBN 978-1-4222-9211-2 (ebook)
  1. 50 Cent (Musician)–Juvenile literature. 2. Rap musicians–United States–Biography–Juvenile literature. I. Title. II. Title: Fifty Cent.
  ML3930.A13H55 2012
  782.421649092–dc22
  [B]
                          2011005802

Produced by Harding House Publishing Services, Inc.
www.hardinghousepages.com
Interior Design by MK Bassett-Harvey.
Cover design by Torque Advertising & Design.

Publisher's notes:
  • All quotations in this book come from original sources and contain the spelling and grammatical inconsistencies of the original text.
  • The Web sites mentioned in this book were active at the time of publication. The publisher is not responsible for Web sites that have changed their addresses or discontinued operation since the date of publication. The publisher will review and update the Web site addresses each time the book is reprinted.

DISCLAIMER: The following story has been thoroughly researched, and to the best of our knowledge, represents a true story. While every possible effort has been made to ensure accuracy, the publisher will not assume liability for damages caused by inaccuracies in the data, and makes no warranty on the accuracy of the information contained herein. This story has not been authorized nor endorsed by 50 Cent.

Contents

Hip-Hop lingo

An **album** is a group of songs together on one CD.

Rap is a kind of music where rhymes are chanted, often with music in the background. When people **rap**, they make up these rhymes, sometimes off the top of their heads.

Lyrics are the words in a song.

A **nightclub** is a place where people dance and drink alcohol.

A **live show** is when a musician performs in front of a group of people.

A **soundtrack** is a collection of all the songs on a movie.

A **contract** is a written agreement between two people. Once you've signed a contract, it's against the law to break it. When a musician signs a contract with a music company, the musician promises to give all her music to that company for them to produce as CDs and sell—and the music company promises to pay the musician a certain amount of money. Usually, a contract is for a certain period of time.

Debut is another word for first.

Critics are people who judge artistic works and say what is good and what is bad about them.

'Hood is another way to say neighborhood. It's usually used in cities.

A **label** is a company that produces music and sells CDs.

Chapter 1

Get Rich or Die Trying!

50 Cent came out of nowhere. One day no one knew his name. The next day, everyone was talking about him. One day he was selling drugs on the street. The next day, he was one of the best known names in hip-hop. And it all happened before his first **album** ever came out!

Hip-hop has lots of "gangstas." Gangstas are tough rappers. They **rap** about crime, guns, and drugs. Lots of people call themselves gangstas, but not everyone really is. 50 Cent is one of the few real ones. He went through some rough stuff as a kid.

50 dealt drugs as a teenager. He got arrested and went to jail. At one point, he faced up to nine years in jail. He was only eighteen years old when that happened.

Things didn't get easier when he became a rapper. He stopped dealing drugs, but life stayed dangerous. Someone shot him with nine bullets, but he survived. Then someone stabbed him. He survived that too.

Anyone can rap about killing and drugs. But when 50 raps about that stuff, he raps from experience.

Starting on the Streets

In 2003, very few rap fans outside of New York City had heard of 50 Cent. He had a lot of fans in his hometown, though. He grew up in Queens, New York. He made some mixtapes and passed them around the neighborhood. Mixtapes are albums made at home. Usually they're not very expensive to make. They let musicians record their music without paying a studio to do it.

These mixtapes became popular. People liked 50's **lyrics**. He sold his mixtapes wherever people would buy them. He sold them on street corners and at **nightclubs**. Sometimes nightclubs paid him to do **live shows**.

Even with all the attention in his hometown, 50 Cent didn't become famous. Lucky for him, the rapper Eminem heard 50's music.

Eminem heard something special in 50's music. He saw that 50 had a chance at being one of the best in hip-hop. He thought 50 sounded like the rappers Tupac and Notorious B.I.G. Both those rappers died in the 1990s. They had grown up with violence and drugs, just like 50.

Eminem wanted to help the young rapper. So he gave him the chance of his life.

Getting Rich

Eminem made a movie called *8 Mile*. It was a movie about his life. He decided to use some of 50's songs for the **soundtrack**. Things were going great for 50. But then they got even better.

Eminem offered 50 Cent a **contract** worth more than $1 million! For an unknown rapper, this was tons of money. 50 was very happy. Right away, Eminem's **label** told everyone that 50 grew up a gangsta. People thought gangstas were good rappers. The label wanted to get people excited about 50's **debut** album.

It worked. People were very excited about 50's first album. Someone stole the album from the studio before it was finished. People bought it on the street and downloaded it on the Internet. 50's album got popular before it even went to stores.

But 50 wasn't mad. He loved it! People stealing his record just meant people wanted to buy it. He was right. When the CD came out, it sold almost one million copies in one week! Stores couldn't keep enough copies on the shelves. By the end of the year, the album had gone platinum six times. Platinum means selling one million copies. 50 had sold six million!

Famed rapper Eminem and legendary music producer Dr. Dre flank 50 Cent at the 2004 Shady National Convention. Eminem discovered 50 Cent and convinced Dr. Dre to share the expense of signing him to a contract and producing his first album.

He called the album *Get Rich or Die Trying.* The title seemed to make sense. He had been shot and stabbed. Now he was rich.

All Gangsta

What made 50 so successful? Well, he rapped about stuff that really happened to him. He wasn't pretending. People connected to the songs on *Get Rich.*

Critics loved *Get Rich or Die Tryin'.* When critics and fans both like your music, you're in luck. 50's music career was off to a great start.

His most popular song was "In Da Club." It talked about leaving the streets. It told about becoming rich. 50 said the song told

50 Cent shakes hands with Jimmy Iovine, the chairman of Interscope Records. Interscope promotes and distributes albums for Shady Records and Aftermath Entertainment, the labels that offered 50 Cent a $1 million bonus for his 2003 debut album.

This image shows the cover of 50 cent's first album, *Get Rich or Die Tryin'*. The bullet hole on the cover references the many times that 50 Cent has been shot. Marketing experts used his experiences to show audiences that he was a real gangsta.

how people think in the **'hood**. Where 50 came from, everyone is poor. Everyone wants to get rich.

50's story is a true "rags to riches" tale. He went from having nothing, to having everything. Only two months after his first album, he was a multi-millionaire. But things hadn't always been so great for 50.

Hip-Hop lingo

Potential is someone's power to do something he hasn't done yet.

A **studio** is a place where musicians go to record their music and turn it into CDs.

A **stage name** is a different name that musicians use when they are performing or selling music.

Chapter 2

From the Streets to Stardom

50 Cent's real name is Curtis James Jackson III. He was born in South Jamaica, a poor neighborhood in Queens, New York. The streets of South Jamaica were Curtis's whole world. He rarely left the neighborhood. And he never left the city.

He was born on July 6, 1975. His mom's name was Sabrina Jackson. Curtis was born when Sabrina was only fifteen years old. He never knew his father. Sabrina never talked about him.

After Curtis was born, Sabrina brought him to live with her parents. She was the youngest of nine kids. The house was very crowded. Sabrina left to live in her own house and started selling drugs. Curtis stayed with his grandparents.

Curtis had no dad. Now he hardly ever saw his mom.

Curtis and His Mom

Curtis's mom was never mean to him. She just wasn't around much. She was a teenager when Curtis was born. She was still very young.

She started selling drugs to make money. At first, Curtis didn't know how his mom got cash. He loved the times when she came to visit him. She always brought a gift. Sometimes she brought a toy. Sometimes it was clothing. Sometimes it was just cash. In the book 50 Cent wrote about his life, he tells about his mom's visits. "Every visit was like Christmas," he wrote.

Curtis remembers the bike she gave him when he was six. By that time, he knew his mom sold drugs. He knew the bike was from someone who bought drugs from his mom. The person couldn't pay his mom in cash so they gave her the bike. Curtis didn't care, though. He loved the bike more because of that. He knew that his mom was thinking about him while she worked.

In the movie *Get Rich or Die Tryin'*, Marc John Jefferies plays young Marcus, the character modeled after 50 Cent. In this scene Marcus is being scolded for misbehaving by his mother, played by Viola Davis.

Then a horrible thing happened. When Curtis was just eight years old, his mom died. She was murdered during a drug deal. 50 remembers his grandfather crying when he told him the bad news. 50 wrote about it in his book: "Even at eight years old, you know what it means when you hear your mother isn't coming back. It meant that Christmas was over."

Selling Drugs

Things started to go bad for Curtis after his mom died. He misbehaved in school. He began to look up to drug dealers in his neighborhood. Curtis knew these men sold drugs. He also knew they were rich. They had nice things and drove cool cars. 50 wanted that life.

So when he turned eleven, he started selling too. He sold drugs after school hours, when his grandparents thought he was playing games in the street. Curtis picked it up quick. He learned everything he needed to know in under a year. The more he did it, the easier it got.

Curtis sold a lot of drugs. By the time he was in high school, he was making lots of money, too. He knew the best spots to sell. His favorite place was the main street in South Jamaica. Then, like most drug dealers who sell a lot of drugs, he got arrested.

He was seventeen years old. He was young. Instead of jail time, the court sent him to rehab. Rehab is a place where people get help with drugs or crime.

But rehab didn't help Curtis. He wanted to keep selling drugs. In his book he wrote, "I got the itch. I wanted to be back on the strip, selling. Like, not *now* but *RIGHT now*."

That's exactly what he did. As soon as he got out of rehab, he started selling again. He went right back to his old ways. He forgot everything he learned in rehab about how drugs are bad. There was too much money to be made. Soon he hired a few kids from the 'hood to work for him.

Curtis was not even twenty years old, and yet he was selling over $5,000 of drugs a day. But he couldn't get away with it forever.

Shock Treatment

Once again, the police caught Curtis. This time he faced up to nine years in jail. But the judge offered him a deal. He could avoid jail if he joined a program called "Shock." The "Shock" program is like boot camp in the army. The prisoners are like soldiers. They wake up before dawn and live in freezing cold weather. They do very hard work. In six months, they work over 650 hours!

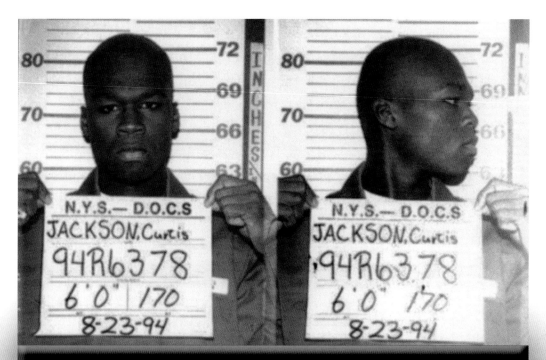

These mug shots were taken when Curtis was arrested for dealing drugs in 1994. Rather than go to jail, Jackson chose to attend a "boot camp" program meant to rehabilitate him. Once his scentence was finished, though, he returned to his criminal lifestyle.

Curtis made it through boot camp. But he didn't change his ways. When he got home, he started selling again. It was going to take more than hard work and cold weather to stop him from selling drugs. But this time he told himself he'd only sell drugs for a little while. Only until he found another way to make money.

Then Curtis got a surprise. His girlfriend got pregnant. He was going to be a daddy! The news changed everything for Curtis. He knew that if he kept selling, he'd be arrested. He'd go to jail. He didn't want his kid to grow up without a dad, like he had. He didn't want his kid to grow up around drugs, like he had.

In 1997, his girlfriend, Tanisha, gave birth to a baby boy. They named him Marquise. Curtis and Tanisha never married. But Curtis decided on that day to be a good dad. He gave up selling drugs. Now there was another question—what would he do instead?

Becoming a Rapper

Curtis always liked hip-hop music. He was like most kids who grow up on the streets. He especially liked gangsta rap. Gangsta rap talked about stuff that actually happened to Curtis and his friends.

Sometimes Curtis made mixtapes with his friends. That's how he found out he had a talent for rapping. But just having talent isn't enough. If you want to get rich, you have to know the right people.

For Curtis, the right person turned out to be Jason Mizell. Mizell was also known as Jam Master Jay. He was a member of one of rap's most famous groups, Run-D.M.C. Jason heard one of Curtis's mixtapes and loved it. He knew that this young man had talent. He had **potential**.

So he made an offer to Curtis. The only recordings of his rapping that Curtis owned sounded very rough. Jam Master Jay couldn't pay him for his music. But he could make new recordings for him.

He could make his music sound even better. Jay brought Curtis to his personal **studio**. There, they made better recordings of Curtis's songs.

With better-sounding songs, Curtis sold more mixtapes. He even sold them to radio stations. He became one of the most popular rappers in New York City. And he did it all by word of mouth.

50 Cent Lives On

Curtis began to search for a **stage name**. It's normal in hip-hop to use a stage name for rapping. He decided on the name "50 Cent." The name had once belonged to Kelvin Darnell Martin.

Martin or "50 Cent" was a famous drug dealer from Curtis's neighborhood. He'd been murdered in 1987. It was a short name and easy to remember. And the memory of Martin gave the name street cred. This meant that it was a name that people from the 'hood would know. Martin was respected on the streets. Curtis decided to use his name. By doing so, he kept Martin's memory alive.

50 Cent's Big Break

Things were going well for 50. He had a new sound and a new name. Then he got his big break. Columbia Records called. They wanted to offer him a record deal. He went into their studio and began to record *Power of the Dollar.* It would be his first real album.

50 was so close to making his dream come true. But then it happened. He was sitting outside his grandmother's house one night in his car. Suddenly, another car pulled up. Someone fired a gun at 50's car. Nine bullets hit him. One shot hit his mouth and knocked out one of his teeth.

There was good news and bad news. The good news—he survived. He told police that the shooting might have been payback. 50 had made a lot of enemies as a drug dealer. The bad news—Columbia didn't want to make 50's album anymore.

50 Cent is pictured here with his nine-year-old son, Marquise Jackson, as they attend the *Child Magazine* 2006 fashion show in New York City. The birth of his son made Curtis consider changing his lifestyle.

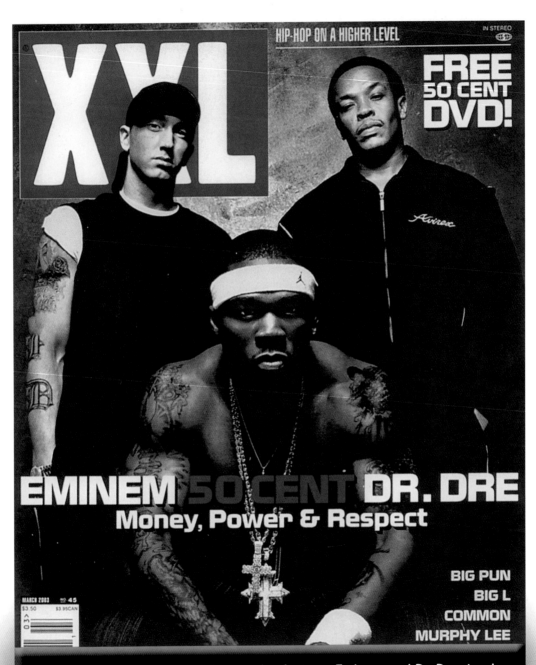

IN STEREO

XXL

FREE 50 CENT DVD!

EMINEM 50 CENT DR. DRE
Money, Power & Respect

BIG PUN
BIG L
COMMON
MURPHY LEE

MARCH 2003   45

$3.50 $3.95CAN

The March 2003 issue of *XXL* magazine features Eminem and Dr. Dre standing behind their new star, 50 Cent. The title "Money, Power & Respect" sums up the attitude that 50 seeks to inject into his music.

Eminem to the Rescue

50 was really sad. He had put all his hopes on that album. So he was surprised when Eminem called him. Eminem had heard his mixtapes and loved them. He offered to help 50 become a star.

Hip-Hop lingo

Promoting something means helping to sell it. It usually means wearing or using a product on TV or in public.

A **role model** is someone whom kids can look up to and try to be like.

Solo means by yourself. A solo artist sings by himself instead of with a group.

Chapter 3

Rap Superstar

With the help of Eminem, 50's first album became a hit. *Get Rich or Die Tryin'* played on radio stations across the world. 50's future looked bright. But even with the whole world in his hands, 50 struggled. Even at the top, there were troubles.

Violent Past

50's past still haunted him. After his album came out, he stopped selling drugs. But he still got in trouble with the law. In 2003, police found a gun in his car. But the gun wasn't his, so he didn't go to jail.

It didn't stop there. In 2004, people accused 50 of beating up a fan at a show. 50 was guilty of the crime. The judge didn't send him to jail though. He told 50 to stay out of trouble for the next two years. He said 50 was a **role model** and should behave better.

Grammys Got No Love for 50

Grammy Awards are given every year to musicians. It's a big honor to receive a Grammy. People predicted that 50 Cent would get at least one.

After losing the Best New Artist Grammy to rock group Evanescence, 50 Cent surprised the audience by going onto the stage in protest. The incident of poor sportsmanship earned him criticism from veiwers and commentators, who felt he should have stayed in his seat.

But they were wrong. 50 didn't win a single Grammy in 2004. This surprised a lot of people, including 50. He didn't take the loss well. He came on stage during someone else's speech. This took attention away from the real winner of the award. It wasn't one of his best moments. He was behaving rudely, and that didn't make people like him.

New Talent

50 didn't let it slow him down for long. He stayed true to his dream. He wanted to be the best rapper he could be. He also wanted to help other young men like him. So he came up with an idea he called "G-Unit." G-Unit would be a record label and a music group. It would help young rappers make albums.

The young men in G-Unit had been 50's friends for a long time. He'd known them since his childhood in Queens. 50 helped them make their own records. But he also made a group record with them. G-Unit called their first record *Beg for Mercy*. It sold 2.3 million copies.

G-Unit brought in other rappers too. The rap duo Mobb Deep joined G-Unit. Together, they made an album called *Blood Money*. It was a big hit. G-Unit's success proved that 50 was a lot more than a **solo** artist. He had plenty of tricks up his sleeve.

Gettin' Rich

50 saw that selling albums wasn't the only way to make money. Once you get really famous, you don't just sell music. You sell yourself. And that's exactly what 50 did. He became "the face" of many products.

50 Cent and his crew, G-Unit, appear at the NRJ Music Awards in Cannes, France, in 2006. G-Unit is comprised of a number of rappers, including Young Buck, Lloyd Banks, Tony Yayo, and Domination. 50 Cent has helped his G-Unit associates with their own careers.

50 was happy to be used to sell stuff. His first job was **promoting** shoes for Reebok. But Reebok ran into trouble using him as their spokesperson. In England, Reebok couldn't use 50 on their commercials. People said that 50 supported violence. And so Reebok stopped showing the ad.

This was a problem for 50. People liked him because he came from a dangerous world. But many other people didn't approve of that same world. They saw him as a bad person.

While recording vocal parts for his video game, *Bulletproof*, 50 Cent takes a break for a photo. In addition to the rapper's voice, the game also includes many exclusive rap tracks from 50 Cent and other G-Unit rappers.

50 let people think what they wanted about him. He sold a recording of his voice to a ringtone company. He also made a big video game deal. Sierra Entertainment wanted to make a game called *Bulletproof*. The game was about 50's life on the streets.

He promoted a grape-flavored drink for Vitamin Water. And he created his own clothing line. He called it G-Unit Clothing. It made a lot of money. The *New York Times* called 50 one of the hardest-working celebrities. There was no doubt about it—he was going to get rich, or die trying!

Hip-Hop lingo

The **big screen** is the screen in a movie theater.

Chapter 4

Putting the Fear Behind Him

Violence has always been a part of 50's life. From the beginning, he's had to watch his back. But as he got older, he changed his attitude. He didn't want to be just a rich gangsta. A few things helped him change. First, he kept his career growing. Also, some of his enemies got put in jail.

Movie Star

50 wanted to take his career to the next level. He was going to put his life's story up on the **big screen**. And what better name for a movie about 50 Cent than *Get Rich or Die Tryin'*? It was pretty much the theme of his life, after all.

So 50 pulled the trigger on the movie deal. An Irish guy named Jim Sheridan was in charge of it. Sheridan grew up poor, just like 50. He'd seen a lot of tough neighborhoods. Sure, hiring an older white guy to make a movie about 50 Cent seemed weird. But Sheridan was excited, so they started filming.

This scene from *Get Rich or Die Tryin'* shows Marcus (50 Cent) sitting in a cell. Most critics found that 50's acting ability left something to be desired. His voiceovers sounded vacant, and they felt his acting did not show emotional depth.

Sheridan believed in 50. He wanted 50 to play himself in the movie. It was a big challenge for the rapper. He'd never acted before. But Sheridan believed he could do it. He told 50 to just be himself.

Sadly, it didn't work out too well. People didn't think 50 did a good job acting. Even worse, the movie didn't make much money. 50's fans all came out to see the movie. But no one else did.

Even so, the movie proved that 50 DID have a lot of fans. It also proved he had the potential to become an even bigger star. Other movie deals were definitely on the way. It wasn't a total failure.

The Murder Inc. Trial

Meanwhile, a pretty big trial was going down in a New York City courtroom. A drug dealer named Kenneth "Supreme" McGriff was on trial. People said that Supreme was a pretty bad guy. At the time, he was accused of killing two people. Later, in 2007, a judge said he was guilty. He gave McGriff a life-sentence in jail.

How did it connect to 50? Because people accused McGriff of a lot of bad things, including the attempt on 50's life in 2000. They said McGriff and two men fired shots at 50. They almost killed him in his car, outside his grandparents' house, the time he was shot nine times but survived. 50 had never known who attacked him that night. Now he did.

McGriff didn't go to jail for attacking 50. He went to jail for the murder of two other men. Even so, it was a big step for 50. One of his worst enemies was behind bars. He could now sleep a little bit easier. He could move on with his life.

50's Secret Weapon

While filming *Get Rich or Die Tryin'*, 50 found time to make another album. He called it *The Massacre*. It was his first solo album since *Get Rich*. People were excited to hear it, especially his most hardcore fans. They'd waited a long time, almost three years.

50 tried different styles in *The Massacre*. He decided he'd already done gangsta rap. He'd already rapped about gunshots and drugs. 50 realized that life on the streets was more than just that stuff. People from his old 'hood feel the same emotions everyone else does. They have fun. They feel pain. They enjoy parties and worry about their kids.

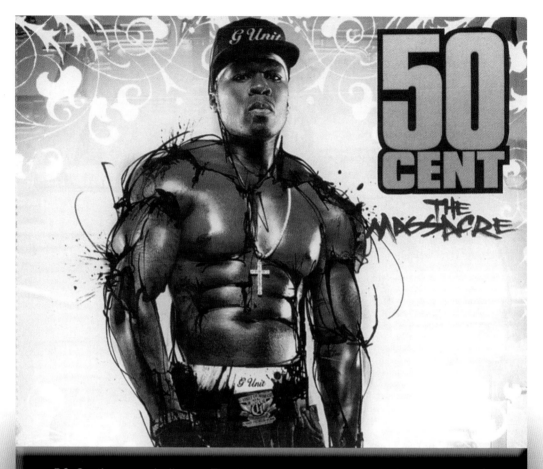

50 Cent's second album, *The Massacre*, was released in 2005. Although generally not considered as good as *Get Rich or Die Tryin'*, *The Massacre* did reach number one on both the American and British charts.

It was time to branch out. 50 wanted to make music for all moods. He didn't like the image of himself as an angry gangsta. In the book he wrote about himself, he says, "I couldn't pretend like I was Angry Man all the time. When someone's feeling happy, I should have a song for them."

Critics said *The Massacre* wasn't as good as *Get Rich*. But that didn't hurt its sales. The new album reached number one in both America and England! 50 had done it again. He'd made another number-one album.

50 Cent Style

50 definitely had his own style. Critics said 50 acted like music was no big deal. They said he acted like he could be or do anything. 50 confused people. He acted like he could be a drug dealer. Or a rich business man. In reality, it was all part of his image. He wanted people to think he didn't try hard. The truth was he worked very hard to be a success.

50 gives everything to his music. It's his life. His hard work has taken him far in life. His "never-give-up" attitude would help him in the future.

Hip-Hop lingo

Feuding is fighting between two people or groups that goes on a long time.

A **truce** is when two sides agree to stop fighting.

Charity is doing something to help make people's lives better.

Obesity means being overweight.

Chapter 5

Rapping into the Future

The next few years were busy ones for 50. He made three albums between 2005 and 2009. He became one of the richest rappers in the game. But he was more than just rich. He was famous, too. He became one of the most important rappers of the day. After almost ten years of success, 50 had earned some respect.

More Grammy Letdowns

The Massacre brought 50 a lot of money. But it didn't bring him a Grammy. His fans loved it, but the judges didn't. Sadly, 50 was once again beaten at the 2006 Grammys. The award for Best Rapper went to Kanye West.

Keeping the Peace

This time, 50 didn't let the Grammys get him down. He was busy **feuding** with another rapper. He was upset with The Game, one of the guys in G-Unit. 50 had taken The Game under his wing and helped him. He had worked on The Game's album to make it better. The album became very popular. But 50 said The Game didn't give 50 enough credit. Their argument turned into a feud.

Then it became violent. Someone fired shots outside 50's office in NYC. No one was hurt. But everyone learned a lesson. It was time to call a **truce** before things got worse.

So 50 Cent and The Game made a big move. They decided to show their peaceful feelings with some **charity**. They gave money to the Boys Choir of Harlem. 50 gave $150,000 to the group. The Game gave $103,500. The Boys Choir taught kids how to sing. Giving it money proved that 50 and The Game cared about music. It also showed that the two rappers cared about peace. They didn't want any more violence.

More Charity

50's charity plans didn't stop there. He had more plans to make the world a better place. He created two charities. One gives money to kids from his old high school. His school is very poor, and the charity helps kids graduate. The other charity helps in the fight against childhood **obesity**.

Why obesity? Because 50 struggled with it when he was young. No one thinks of 50 as being overweight. The photos of him on album covers show a powerful man. He has tons of muscles. He looks thin and strong. Few people know that 50 has fought obesity for most of his life.

It started when he was a kid. He had bad eating habits. He told the Associated Press, "I had all the unhealthy habits. Soda . . . a lot of fast food, all those things." Then he changed his habits and started exercising. He became much healthier. But he remembers how it felt to be overweight.

50 decided he could help fight childhood obesity. He agreed to sponsor a competition. The competition had young chefs cre-

ate healthy foods. The goal was to make healthy meals for school lunches. The winner received $100,000 for college!

In 2011, 50 started selling an energy drink called Street King. Money made from sales of the drink would go to help get food to children in Africa. 50 understands that giving back to others is an important part of being successful!

Deshaun "Proof" Holton (left) performs with Mekhi Phifer and Eminem in 2002. The April 2006 murder of Proof caused some people to examine the link between violence and hip-hop. 50 Cent, for one, believes the music does not cause or endorse violence.

This frame from *The Simpsons* shows the cartoon version of 50 Cent standing behind juvenile bad boy Bart Simpson. The rapper appeared in an episode called "Pranksta Rap," in which Bart feigns kidnapping to avoid being punished for attending a 50 Cent concert.

Rap and Violence

Violence shook the hip-hop world again in 2006. Thankfully, this time 50 wasn't involved. A rapper called Proof was killed in a nightclub. He was shot in a gunfight.

Reporters asked 50 about Proof's death. They asked him if he thought gangsta rap was too violent. 50 agreed that gangsta rap is violent. But he didn't think gangsta rap made people kill each other. He said that parents should teach their kids about music. He said parents should tell their kids not to take music too seriously.

50 said violence in America has nothing to do with hip-hop. He said that violence goes deeper. It's a part of people's lives.

New Man, New Skills

In 2006, 50 acted in another movie. He wanted to show people that he took acting seriously. The movie was called *Home of the Brave*. It was about soldiers in Iraq.

At the time, people had lots of questions about the Iraq War. It was an unpopular war. People worried about Iraq and our soldiers there. 50 got to be a part of an important movie. It was one of the first to show the effects of the Iraq War on soldiers.

It was a chance for 50 to show people another side of himself. He didn't want to just be "gangsta 50." He was tired of being seen that way. He said, "My past is my shadow. It follows me everywhere I go. All those things come from when I had no choice. They put my back against the wall, I gotta do what I gotta do."

50 wanted a new start. He wanted a chance to rise above the violence of the past. Movies like *Home of the Brave* helped him do just that. He continues to get acting parts in movies. He acted in *Righteous Kill* with famous actors Al Pacino and Robert De Niro. He also appeared on the cartoon *The Simpsons*. He recorded the voice of himself for the episode "Pranksta Rap."

50 doesn't plan on quitting acting anytime soon. In 2007, he started his own film company. No surprise, he called it G-Unit Films.

Curtis

Of course, music remained 50's main interest. He went back to his roots for his next album. He even recorded some songs in his old house in Queens! In the old days, everyone called him Curtis. He called the album *Curtis* because it connected him to his past. 50 wanted to get back to what made him into the man he is today.

Curtis had two goals. One was to help 50 appreciate his life. He had become so rich, so fast. Going back home helped him remember what it was like to be poor. But it also helped him write new music. He listened to the city streets. He connected to the energy that inspired him as a young man.

Before I Self Destruct

50 released his fourth album in 2009. He called it *Before I Self Destruct*. The album had a new goal. People thought *Curtis* was too soft. They thought 50 had lost his edge. So 50 focused on his dark side in *Self Destruct*.

With *Curtis*, 50 went back to his roots. He remembered where he came from as a person. With *Self Destruct*, 50 went back to his musical roots. He wanted to get back to the magic of *Get Rich*. So he used more gangsta themes. He tried to get back some of his "tough guy" cred. 50 wanted to let people know that he had changed—but not completely!

In 2011, 50 told fans that he'd started working on his next album. He also put out songs for free on the Internet to help spread the word about his new album and his Street King energy drink. Fans couldn't wait to hear more songs from 50 Cent no matter how he put them out!

Writing Books

50 has written a number of books. His first was the story of his own life. It was called *From Pieces to Weight: Once Upon a Time in Southside Queens*. It tells how 50 got where he is today.

He also wrote *The Ski Mask Way*. It's a book about a small-time drug dealer who tries to rob his boss. 50 planned to turn into a movie.

50 wrote another book called *The 50th Law*. To write it, he teamed up with Robert Greene. Greene had written a book called *The 33 Strategies of War*. It was a very popular book in the hip-hop world. 50 admired Greene and wanted to meet him. So they did. The two men decided to write a book together.

The 50th Law is about having no fear. They call it "fearlessness" in the book. Greene says 50 is an example of a power figure. A power figure is someone who takes control when everything is a mess. A power figure is not afraid. Hustling on the streets taught 50 a lot about being fearless. Much of the book is about lessons learned from the streets.

For the Fans

50 admits that he isn't the best role model for kids. His life is full of violence and bad choices. But he knows he's come a long way. In his book, he writes:

"I am truly blessed. And I remind myself every day that if I'm in a good space now, it's because I been in a bad space for so long before. I don't consider myself a role model, because I think a role model should be speaking and saying something positive all the time. That ain't me. But my story has to be an inspiration to people that's from the bottom, people that's from the same walks of life I'm from. I'm proof that success is possible. They can look at me and say, I know *I* could do this, because *he* did *that*."

Time Line

1975 Curtis James Jackson III is born on July 6 in South Jamaica, Queens.

1983 Curtis's mother Sabrina Jackson is murdered in a drug deal.

1986 Curtis (50 Cent) begins dealing drugs.

1991 Curtis (50 Cent) drops out of high school to sell drugs full time.

1992 Curtis (50 Cent) is arrested for drug possession and sentenced to two years in a residential rehabilitation program.

1994 Curtis (50 Cent) is arrested for drug dealing; he is sentenced to six months in a military-style outdoors boot camp.

1996 50 Cent meets Jam Master Jay, who teaches him to rap and demands that he give up drug dealing.

2000 50 Cent signs a contract with Columbia Records to record *Power of the Dollar* but loses the contract when he is shot and wounded.

2002 50 Cent records three songs for the soundtrack to Eminem's film *8 Mile*.

2003 50 Cent releases *Get Rich or Die Tryin'*, which becomes wildly successful and leads to three hit singles.

2004 50 Cent is arrested for assault in a Massachusetts nightclub. He pleads guilty and is placed on probation.

2005 50 Cent plays the lead role in the film version of *Get Rich or Die Tryin'* and releases *The Massacre*.

2005   50 Cent publishes a book about his life, called *From Pieces to Weight: Once Upon a Time in Southside Queens.*

2006   50 Cent films the Iraq War drama *Home of the Brave.*

2007   50 Cent releases his third studio album, called *Curtis.*

2009   50 Cent releases his fourth studio album, *Before I Self Destruct.*

2010   50 wins his first Grammy, Best Rap Performance by a Duo or Group, for his song "Crack A Bottle" with Eminem and Dr. Dre.

2011   50 Cent announces his next album will come out in 2012.

          50 starts selling Street King energy drink to raise money for charity.

Discography
Solo Albums

2000   Power of the Dollar (unreleased)

2003   Get Rich or Die Tryin'

2005   The Massacre

Get Rich or Die Tryin' (film soundtrack)

2007   Curtis

2009   Before I Self Destruct

Albums with G-Unit

2003   Beg for Mercy

2008   Terminate on Sight

In Books

Baker, Soren. *The History of Rap and Hip Hop*. San Diego, Calif.: Lucent, 2006.

Comissiong, Solomon W. F. *How Jamal Discovered Hip-Hop Culture*. New York: Xlibris, 2008.

Cornish, Melanie. *The History of Hip Hop*. New York: Crabtree, 2009.

Czekaj, Jef. *Hip and Hop, Don't Stop!* New York: Hyperion, 2010.

Haskins, Jim. *One Nation Under a Groove: Rap Music and Its Roots*. New York: Jump at the Sun, 2000.

Hatch, Thomas. *A History of Hip-Hop: The Roots of Rap*. Portsmouth, N.H.: Red Bricklearning, 2005.

Websites

50 Cent's Facebook Page
www.facebook.com/50cent

50 Cent's Official Website
www.50cent.com

Starpulse 50 Cent Page
www.starpulse.com/Music/50_Cent

VH1's Official Artist Profile for 50 Cent
www.vh1.com/artists/az/50_cent/artist.jhtml

Website for the Film *Get Rich or Die Tryin'*
www.getrichordietryinmovie.com

Index

About the Author

Z.B. Hill is a an author and publicist living in Binghamton, New York. He has a special interest in adolescent education and how music can be used in the classroom.

Picture Credits

1: Dreamstime.com, Sbukley
6: Suzan/AAD/Star Max
9: Dara Kushner/INFGoff
10: PRNewsFoto/NMI
11: Michelle Feng/NMI
12: Feature Photo Service/NMI
14: Paramount Pictures/LILO/SIPA
16: Zuma Press/NMI
19: Elizabeth Lippman/Splash News
20: Michelle Feng/NMI
22: AFP/Gerard Julien
24: AP Photo/Kevork Djansezian
25: Pat Denton/WENN
26: Feature Photo Service/NMI
28: Paramount Pictures/LILO/SIPA
30: Paramount Pictures/NMI
32: Michelle Feng/NMI
34: Niviere/NMA06/SIPA
37: KRT/Mandi Wright
38: Fox Broadcasting/NMI

To the best knowledge of the publisher, all other images are in the public domain. If any image has been inadvertently uncredited, please notify Harding House Publishing Services, Vestal, New York 13850, so that rectification can be made for future printings.